A SHORT HISTO

HERNE
HILL

Researched and written by
John Brunton

THE HERNE HILL SOCIETY

First published in July 2011 for The Herne Hill Society
PO Box 27845
London SE24 9XA

Reprinted with corrections July 2011

Composed in Arno Pro and Charlemagne

ISBN: 978 1 873 520833

CONTENTS

INTRODUCTION AND ACKNOWLEDGEMENTS

Original enamel Southern Region station sign

Many local residents will be familiar with **The Book of Herne Hill**, written by one of the Society's founder members, Patricia Jenkyns, and published in 2003; but it is a long book, now out of print. Newcomers to the area have asked if there is a booklet about the history of the area. Here it is.

This booklet looks at the history of the area as far as is known from the 12th century, concentrating on the 19th century onwards when most of Herne Hill was built. It looks at the development of the area, the importance of transport links and local attractions, and is comprehensively illustrated with maps, photos and drawings.

John Brunton, who has helped to write several of the Society's recent publications, carried out the initial research and prepared the text for publication. Nick Baker made the design and layout.

The Society acknowledges the assistance of the editorial panel: David Taylor, Pat Roberts, Colin Wight, Nick Baker and is grateful for the comments on the draft made by Jeffrey Doorn, Robert Holden and George Young.

WHERE IS HERNE HILL?

Herne Hill, about 4 miles (6.5 kilometres) south of central London, is a well established residential area developed mainly in the years between 1880 and 1920. It may not have the elegant Georgian charm of Dulwich or the edgy vibrancy of Brixton, but situated almost equidistant between those rather better-known areas, it has its own history and character.

To the west is Brixton, to the east is Dulwich, and Tulse Hill is to the south. But there are no specific boundaries to Herne Hill. The London SE24 postal district is a good fit. But there are people living in SE21, SE5 or SW2 who would also identify with Herne Hill. So if you think you live in Herne Hill, you probably do! Now shared between the London boroughs of Southwark and Lambeth, Herne Hill was in the County of Surrey until it came under the control of the London County Council in 1889.

Detail from John Rocque 1746

WHY THE NAME?

No one really knows. Perhaps it is called after *le Herne*, the name of a field in
Brixton; or it may be that the river Effra, which flows through the heart of
Herne Hill but is sadly now underground, attracted large numbers of herons
(*herne* in Middle English). Another possible interpretation is "hill by a nook of
land" deriving from the Old English *hyrne* (corner or angle) *hyll*. Alternatively,
it may have been named after George or Benjamin Herne who were
prominent Dulwich residents in the 17th century.

... AND WHEN?

A map published around 1610 by Speed shows the
area as King's Hill. Over 100 years later, John
Rocque's 1746 map gives the name as Island
Green. Bennost's 1758 map does not give a name
but calls the area to the north Dulwich Hill. It has
been suggested that the first reference to *Hearne*
(sic) Hill was in 1789. However, this has not been
confirmed and the first so far substantiated
mention is in Holden's Directory of London

(1802), which refers to a John Davis, paper-stainer, of Herne Hill, Dulwich.

WHO OWNED HERNE HILL?

From the Manorial records that survived the medieval period, there were two
manors in Herne Hill, both owned by monasteries until their dissolution in *c*
1538. One other manor covered lands now in Dulwich. The present Brockwell
Park and part of Tulse Hill to the west was the Manor of Bodley, Upgrove and
Scarlettes. It was held by the Hospital of St Thomas the Martyr, Southwark
from 1352. In 1540 it was passed at first to the Leigh family, then to the Tulse,
Onslow and Winter families until 1807 when it was eventually divided into
two. In 1809 John Blades purchased the half known as Brockwell Park. In the
12th century, Herne Hill became part of the Manor of Milkwell, within the
much larger Manor of Lambeth, the name Milkwell probably referring to the

colour of the water from a spring in the area. It was in the overall ownership of the Archbishop of Canterbury, who in 1197 was receiving an annual rent from Milkwell of six shillings and eight pence. Except during the Commonwealth period, it remained the Archbishop's property until 1862.

In 1291 Milkwell was recorded as belonging to the Hospital of St Thomas, Southwark. In 1305 Edward I granted the Manor to the monastery and

Sir Thomas Wyatt

hospital of St Mary Overie Priory, at a yearly rent of 10 shillings. In 1541, after the Dissolution of the Monasteries, the Manor came under the Crown. Henry VIII then granted it to Sir Thomas Wyatt (1521-54), soldier, courtier and rebel. However 10 years later Sir Thomas was beheaded by Queen Mary for high treason, having led an insurrection against her.

Under Elizabeth I the lease for the land was assigned to Gregory Raylton (d. 1561), one of the Clerks of the Signet to the Queen. It then passed to John Bower, and later came under the control of Thomas Duke. Thomas Duke's heir, Sir Edward Duke, then sold a small part of the Manor to Edward Alleyn of Dulwich. The remainder went to Robert Cambell, a City of London Alderman. However, after the end of the Civil War and the establishment of the Commonwealth in 1649, along with all the other property of the Archbishop of Canterbury, the lands were seized by Parliament. The estates were returned to the new Archbishop following the 1660 Restoration.

In 1691 Robert Cambell's grandson, who had inherited 124 acres of that part of the Manor comprising Herne Hill and Denmark Hill, then sold his share to John Godschall, a London merchant, for £3,680. The Godschall family continued to hold this land until 1783, when William Godschall sold it to Samuel Sanders, a wealthy timber merchant.

GRAND HOUSES

For centuries there has been a road from Camberwell over the hill to the Herne Hill valley. At the northern foot of the hill was Camberwell Lane (now Coldharbour Lane), and on its crest Ashpole Lane, now Red Post Hill. In the valley, there were roads that led to Dulwich and to Norwood. Another road from Stockwell brought pilgrims following the River Effra along Croxted Lane towards the Pilgrims' Way and Canterbury. The first inn on the site of the present Half Moon Tavern was established in the 17th century, no doubt encouraged by the trade brought by these pilgrims.

Early maps show Herne Hill as thinly populated, apart from the rising ground on the northern side. This is in contrast to surrounding areas such as Dulwich, Brixton and Camberwell, where a number of properties are shown. It is probable that Herne Hill was largely forest and meadow, with perhaps a few scattered dwellings. It was certainly well covered with trees. After the Civil War ended in 1651, much of the forest was cut down and sold for ship building and domestic use. Afterwards the land gradually passed to a mixture of farms, small holdings and woods, but as late as the 1760s it was still very rural, with only a small population.

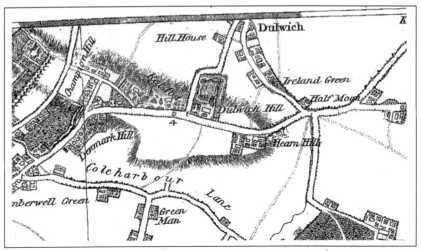

Edwards c1800 (note orientation, south east at top)

Casino House, 1796

The bridges over the Thames at Westminster (1750) and Blackfriars (1769) enabled London to expand south. Houses, shops and businesses grew up along new roads built through open country to villages such as Stockwell, Walworth and Camberwell. For anyone who worked in London, it was too far to walk from Herne Hill. The only means of getting there was by horse and carriage, so only the wealthy could live in Herne Hill.

One of the earliest houses in Herne Hill was Casino (or *Casina*) House, on a site immediately opposite what is now Poplar Walk. It was built in 1796 by Richard Shaw, Solicitor to Warren Hastings, the former Governor-General of Bengal, when Hastings was impeached on charges of mismanagement of funds. The house was the centre of the 15-acre Sunray Estate, of which Sunray Gardens are now all that remains.

A further significant land purchase was in 1809 by the glass maker John Blades of Ludgate Hill. He bought the estate that occupied land which was eventually to form the basis of Brockwell Park. Blades demolished a house located near

Brockwell Hall, 1820

what is now the Norwood Road park boundary and built Brockwell Hall, the mansion that still stands at the top of the hill in Brockwell Park.

The local landowners resisted over-development of the area. They included the Dulwich Estate, who owned the Camberwell side of Herne Hill and Denmark Hill, and Samuel Sanders, who had bought the land fronting onto the northern side of Denmark Hill and Herne Hill. The Dulwich Estate and Sanders' descendants continued to prevent the extensive and crowded housing developments characteristic of the neighbouring areas to the north. They did, however, grant long leases to wealthy people, such as city merchants, businessmen and bankers, who built some large and very fine houses on plots fronting onto Denmark Hill and Herne Hill.

These houses were mostly all detached or semi-detached with large front and back gardens, which helped to preserve the semi-rural atmosphere. By 1843 an almost continuous row of large properties stretched along the western side of the two roads. Looking back on his childhood John Ruskin wrote of Herne Hill: "The view from the ridge on both sides was, before railroads came, entirely lovely: westward at evening, almost sublime, over softly wreathing distances of domestic wood."

Ruskin remembered that when he was about four years old—1819—his father bought "the lease of a house on Herne Hill, a rustic eminence four miles south of the Standard in Cornhill"; of which "the leafy seclusion remains, in all essential points of character, unchanged to this day" (*Praeterita*, 1885-9). Most of these mansions have disappeared, but one or two are still left to show why this area became known as "the Belgravia of South London".

Architects' designs for Herne Hill Villas, c1843

During the 1820s much smaller houses had been built in Regent Row (now Road) to accommodate locally employed labourers and gardeners. Apart from these, Herne Hill remained an affluent rural district of large mansions and gardens, but by the 1860s, except for the large houses along Herne Hill and a few in Half Moon Lane, the area was still mainly fields and farms. Stretching north, on either side along what is now Milkwood Road, were extensive market gardens. These supplied the capital with vegetables and received in return night soil used as a fertiliser.

Herne Hill from Half Moon Lane, 1823

THE RAILWAY ARRIVES

Work began on what is now known as "Poets' Corner", when the former Effra Farm was bought by the Westminster Freehold Land Society in 1855. A slow start was made with laying out the roads (Chaucer, Spenser, Shakespeare and Milton). But with the arrival of the railway, the pace of change quickened and Herne Hill's rural tranquillity began to fade.

In 1862, at the bottom of the hill, Herne Hill station was opened for the London, Chatham and Dover Railway. The first line to open was the route north to Elephant and Castle. By 1864 this had been extended over the Thames to Ludgate Hill (now Blackfriars). The line to Victoria via Brixton also opened in 1862, and was extended south the following year to Dulwich (now West Dulwich), Beckenham and Bromley. In 1869 the line to Tulse Hill was opened to connect with the London, Brighton and South Coast Railway line from London Bridge to Wimbledon and Sutton. Trains were pulled by steam locomotives until the lines were electrified in the 1920s. The station entrance block was listed Grade II in 1999.

Herne Hill Station, 1863

HOMES FOR ALL (WELL, ALMOST)

Railway companies were legally obliged to provide cheap workmen's fares. This meant that people could now live beyond walking distance from where they worked. It led to an enormous expansion of smaller, lower-cost housing for clerks, artisans, craftsmen and their families, the workers taking advantage of cheap fares for commuting into London. By 1911 buyers of workmen's tickets accounted for over 25 percent of all the South Eastern and Chatham Railway's passengers. The popularity of these cheap fares led, in the second half of the 19th century, to the development of working-class suburbs all around London. Often these developments were by private speculative builders. Estates were also developed by philanthropic organisations for people of more modest means. Herne Hill has examples of both types of development.

Dulwich House Estate

This covers the area between Herne Hill and Half Moon Lane and is bounded by Hollingbourne and Danecroft Roads. It was a private development on land owned by the Lett family of timber merchants. The first developments, in 1890/91, were the houses in Warmington Road and Howletts Road. At about the same time, the freehold of the rest of the estate was sold by auction in nine lots and the roads laid out. By 1914 development of this area had almost been completed, with smart late Victorian and Edwardian houses.

Milkwood Estate

This covers the area bounded by Milkwood, Lowden and Poplar Roads. It was built in the 1870s by The Suburban Village and General Dwellings Company, which had been set up to provide decent accommodation for working people. In this the Company was successful, erecting some 570 terraced houses accommodating, in 1901, a population of 3,700. To cater for this increasing population came schools, churches, pubs and shops.

Peabody Estate

The Peabody Trust was founded in 1862 by London-based American banker George Peabody, with the aim of ensuring that as many people as possible had a good home that was safe, warm, clean, light and well maintained. The Rosendale Road Estate was the Trust's first suburban development and also the first to introduce cottage-style housing as well as blocks of flats. In 1899 the Trust bought nearly 20 acres of vacant land off Rosendale Road. By 1902 the four blocks containing 144 flats had been completed. At first the flats were difficult to let and rents had to be reduced, so the Governors decided to develop the rest of the estate with two-storey cottages more suited to a suburban setting. The first group of 82 was completed by 1906. The remaining 64 cottages, designed to a slightly lower standard, were all completed by 1908. Lambeth Council designated the estate a conservation area in 1999.

Peabody Flats, 1902

Springfield Estate

Bounded by Half Moon Lane, Burbage Road and railway lines to the south and west, this area once contained a large mansion, Springfield, built in the 1830s. In 1889 it was demolished. Between 1894 and the early 1900s, the Dulwich Estate Governors (the freeholders) built the houses you see today. They were designed to attract the growing population of middle-class residents, mostly employed in the City and whose sons would perhaps go to Dulwich College.

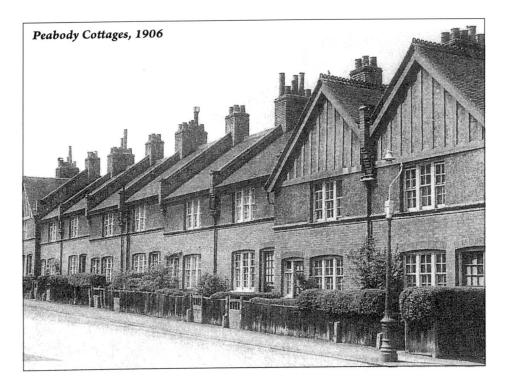

Peabody Cottages, 1906

TOWARDS MODERN TIMES

Horse-drawn tram by the railway bridge, Norwood Road

Regular horse-drawn tram services had arrived in Herne Hill in 1884. From Loughborough Junction trams passed under the railway bridge at Hinton Road and along the length of Milkwood Road. Electrification and double-decker trams came in the early 1900s when the London County Council took over the service. For the number 48 route from Camberwell, the bridge over Hinton Road was too low, and part of Milkwood Road was too narrow to take two tram lines. The route one way was changed to Herne Hill Road, Wanless, Poplar and Lowden Roads, then via Milkwood Road to Herne Hill station and Norwood. Two other tram routes, numbers 33 and 78, ran from Brixton along Effra and Dulwich Roads, to join the number 48 going south along Norwood Road. The trams were phased out by 1952 in favour of buses.

In 1906 the the area's own fire station opened at the bottom of Herne Hill. The original fire engines were horse-drawn and an extra horse had to be on stand-by for use when needed to pull engines up hill. It is said that the land next door (on the site of the former Sorting Office—*c* 1917—and petrol station) was where the fireman's horses grazed. The fire station closed in 1920 and operations were transferred to a new station in West Norwood. In 2003 the building became a branch of Sainsbury's and the fire station sign is still preserved over the shop doorway.

Trams in Milkwood Road

WORLD WAR 1

The war brought many changes to Herne Hill. The newly opened King's College Hospital, which had moved to Denmark Hill from its original Aldwych site in 1913 to become one of London's first teaching hospitals, was taken over by the War Office. It was known as the 4th London General Hospital, and was used as a treatment centre for wounded servicemen. However it also continued to care for the civilian population. A footbridge was built over the railway from the hospital, and Ruskin Park became an annex of King's, with huts for convalescent soldiers. St Saviour's Church in Herne Hill Road formed a club for soldiers' and sailors' wives, and gave concerts to the wounded troops from King's.

King's College Hospital c1916

The Wellcome Physiological Research Laboratories, after 1895, had occupied Brockwell House, worked overtime on antitoxins for diphtheria, typhoid, typhus and anti-gas serums. The laboratories stayed in Brockwell Park until 1922, when they were moved to Beckenham.

As there was no efficient food rationing system there were serious shortages. Many people dug up their flower beds and lawns to plant vegetables, while a large flock of sheep grazed in Brockwell Park. Although there were air raids over London, Herne Hill was not touched. However many local young men and women did not return from war service. A measure of the loss can be gauged from the numbers recorded on the various memorials in Herne Hill.

Sheep grazing in Brockwell Park

On a screen in St Paul's Church are the names of 105 men who lost their lives. In the former St John the Evangelist Church, Guernsey Grove (now the New Testament Church of God), is a memorial to 86 members killed. In the Peabody Estate is a lych gate erected by the tenants to the 35 men from the estate who lost their lives. A fourth memorial used to stand in the Postal Sorting Office, with the names of five employees killed. It was removed after the Sorting Office closed in 2007 and was re-erected in the Camberwell Sorting Office with the support of the Herne Hill Society. A fifth memorial, bearing a single name, was located in the former bank premises at the corner of Herne Hill and Milkwood Road.

Memorial in St John's (right) and the Lych Gate Memorial, Peabody Estate (left).

INTER-WAR YEARS

The inter-war period also saw further housing developments in Herne Hill. For an area so close to central London, the area still had many large houses with large grounds suitable for development.

The former estate of Casino House was bought by the Metropolitan Borough of Camberwell, and the Sunray Estate built in response to the cry for "homes fit for heroes". It comprised 292 dwellings, mainly two-storey houses. Fortunately the south-eastern part of the Sunray estate, with its small lake, was not built on but used to form the very attractive Sunray Gardens. A new road, Dorchester Drive was created in the mid 1930s and a number of attractive houses were built, designed by the well known architects of art deco cinemas, Kemp and Tasker. Each house is different, and No.5, is particularly splendid with fine brickwork and interiors, typical of the time. Dorchester Court, which comprises eight blocks of flats around a central courtyard, was built in 1936 on Herne Hill, on the site formerly occupied by 19th century villas. Dorchester Court and 5 Dorchester Drive are now listed Grade II.

Sunray Estate, "Homes for Heroes"

WORLD WAR 2 AND AFTER

The Second World War saw much damage to Herne Hill, mainly during the 1940-41 Blitz. The railway lines were favourite targets, leading to the destruction of many nearby houses. Few streets escaped damage. Between September 1940 and February 1945 there were nearly 100 civilian deaths and many injuries in Herne Hill as a result of enemy action. Those who lost their lives included four women, a man and a 12-year-old boy when a bomb hit an air-raid shelter in Brockwell Park on 15 September 1940.

After 1945 priority was given to repairing damaged properties. However pre-fabs were also put up – prefabricated houses, factory-built and assembled on site. They contained "all mod cons", including kitchens and bathrooms. Intended only as temporary housing, they proved very popular. In some

Bomb damage in Guernsey Grove

places, such as Myatts Fields in Camberwell, people were still living in pre-fabs until the present century. Later, new houses were built on the cleared bomb-sites. Their designs contrast with neighbouring late Victorian and Edwardian properties. Many large houses were demolished or converted into flats. Some new small blocks of flats were built and, more recently, larger local authority estates of flats and houses, including tower blocks such as those in Dulwich Road.

Milkwood Road was particularly badly affected by bombing – around a quarter of the properties along the railway side had been destroyed or rendered uninhabitable. Most of the remaining houses backing onto the railway were then demolished and the area designated for industrial use. After many years' debate the Mahatma Gandhi Industrial Estate opened for business in 1986. This was followed a few years later by the Dylan Road and Bessemer Park Estates.

HERNE HILL TODAY

Today, Herne Hill is a lively, vibrant and diverse community and much sought after as a place to live, particularly by young families. It has a wide range of independent shops, bars, restaurants and other facilities—as well as its own Lido. Brockwell Park is one of London's premier open spaces. The most recent addition to the area's parks is the award-winning Milkwood Community Park in Milkwood Road.

There are excellent transport links, with bus and rail connections to central London, the City and the West End, as well as south to centres such as Croydon, Bromley and Wimbledon. The Victoria Line station at Brixton is only a short distance away.

Herne Hill has a particularly active local community, supporting a wide range of organisations and Friends' groups, as well as the Herne Hill Society and the Herne Hill Forum, all working to preserve what is best about Herne Hill and to enhance the area for the future.

Some old industries have closed down or moved away. The Fisher Bookbinding firm on the corner of Norwood and Croxted Roads moved away and was developed into flats. The large site formally occupied by Nevill's Bakery in Milkwood Road is now Milkwood Community Park. There are a number of small and medium-sized businesses in the industrial estates along Milkwood Road. The numerous railway arches are home to a variety of light industrial and other activities. Otherwise, employment is in the service sector, shops, restaurants etc. Despite this, Herne Hill is mainly a residential rather

Herne Hill Regeneration Project: Norwood Road and the vista up Brockwell Park, from Railton Road.

than commercial or industrial area, a place where many people find it convenient to live and to travel to work elsewhere. Herne Hill continues to develop. Brockwell Park is being upgraded through a multi-million pound regeneration project, supported by funding from the National Lottery. In December 2010 the completion of the Herne Hill Centre Regeneration Project was celebrated at an inauguration ceremony in the newly pedestrianised area of Railton Road. The event is marked by a plaque on the wall of number 232 Railton Road.

PARKS

Brockwell Park

In 1892 Brockwell Park was established on 78 acres of the original Brockwell Hall estate. A sad aspect of this event was the sudden death at the opening ceremony of Thomas Lynn Bristowe, MP for Norwood. It was through his efforts that the plan to establish the Park had been achieved. Two later land purchases brought the park to its present size.

Brockwell Park c 1900

Milkwood Community Park
This covers part of the site formerly occupied by Nevill's Bakery. The bakery was closed in 1969 and the buildings demolished, together with some of the surrounding houses. The site was kept as a public open space but became derelict. Thanks to the efforts of the local community, led by the Milkwood Residents Association, the money was raised to convert the area to a quality park, with play areas, sports and other facilities. It was formally opened on 19 June 2004.

Ruskin Park
In 1904 part of the land, some 24 acres, belonging to the Sanders Estate and fronting the west side of Denmark Hill, came onto the market. Thanks to the efforts of Frank Trier (1853-1923), a Champion Hill resident, the land was saved from planned housing development and was opened to the public in 1907 as Ruskin Park. Three years later another 12 acres were added to enlarge the park to its present size.

Sunray Gardens
This small but attractive park was formed from the water gardens of the former Casino House. The house was demolished in 1906 and the land bought by the then Camberwell Borough Council. When the Sunray Estate was built in the early 1920s, the Park was preserved, at first as the Casino Open Space then, from 1923, as Sunray Gardens. It was refurbished by Southwark Council in 2001 and is a rare surviving example in London of the work of Humphry Repton, the celebrated landscape designer.

Sunray Gardens

SCHOOLS

The Charter School, Red Post Hill

Opened in 1958, William Penn School for Boys, a Peckham comprehensive high school formed in 1947, closed on this site in 1996. A new Co-educational Community Secondary School opened in 2000 after some building works, for about 1000 students aged between 11 and 18.

Michael Tippett, Heron Road

The original school, Willowfield School, was built in 1976 on the corner of Heron and Milkwood Roads. It was a day school for some 50 boys of secondary school age with emotional or behavioural difficulties. Later girls were admitted. The school closed in 1987 and the buildings demolished. In 2008, the Michael Tippett School, designed by Marks Barfield (who also designed the London Eye) opened on the site.

Bessemer Grange, Dylways

Opened in 1952 to serve the surrounding estate, the school occupies the site of a lake in the former grounds of what was Sir Henry Bessemer's home.

Bessemer Grange

Jessop, Lowden Road

Renamed Jessop School in 1952, Jessop Road School opened in 1876. It was designed to accommodate 552 children (176 boys, 176 girls and 200 infants). It was named after Jessop Road, now disappeared, which ran between Lowden and Milkwood Roads. The present school buildings were erected just before WW2 and further enlarged in the 1960s to accommodate 800 children.

Rosendale Primary, Rosendale Road

The site for this school, located between Rosendale and Turney Roads, was bought in 1894. A temporary iron structure was put up in 1897 to house the school. The present main Junior school buildings were completed in 1900. An Infants school opened in 1908.

St Jude's, Regent Road
The school was built in 1834 to provide a Christian education for the poor of the surrounding area. The site in Railton Road is now occupied by the Temple of Truth Pentecostal Church. The original single-storey building still survives. The school was badly damaged by bombs in 1940 and in 1973 was relocated to its present site in Regent Road.

St Saviour's, Herne Hill Road
The first school building, on the site on Herne Hill Road, was built in 1868 and enlarged in 1892. Up to *c* 1950, it catered for girls and infants. Since the 1950s it has been a Church of England Primary School.

Jessop Road School in the 1930s

CHURCHES

St Paul's

St. Paul's, Herne Hill (C of E)

Herne Hill's parish church was completed in 1844, but destroyed by fire 14 years later. Fortunately it was insured and was rebuilt to the design of GE Street to accommodate 700 people. Local resident John Ruskin who disapproved of the original building welcomed the change. It was listed Grade II in 1954.

St John's, Lowden Road

Opened in 1881, St John's was built to cater for the needs of the expanding population in the surrounding area. The church closed in 1988, but continued to be used by the local community. Strenuous efforts by the Milkwood Residents Association to raise the money to buy the building and retain it for community use have been unsuccessful and, at the time of writing, it is for sale.

Herne Hill Baptist Church

The church hall opened in 1899. The congregation, who since 1897 had been meeting in a railway arch near Loughborough Junction, moved to Half Moon Lane when the building was completed in 1904. It was the first non-conformist church on the Dulwich College Estate and is listed Grade II.

St Saviour's, Herne Hill Road (C of E)

Opened in 1867 to become the Parish Church of St Saviour, it was designed to cater for the area's expanding population but was damaged by bombing in the Blitz. The building was finally demolished in 1981, providing much needed play space for the school. The adjacent parish hall, opened in 1914 to the design of Arthur Beresford Pite, is now used as the church.

Herne Hill United Church, Denmark Hill/Red Post Hill

Built in 1904 as Herne Hill Congregational Church, it suffered from ground settlement, was seriously damaged by a bomb in 1944 and was later demolished, although the hall, built in 1904, is still in use and used by the Herne Hill Society for its monthly meetings. The present church building was opened in 1960. In 1972 the Congregational Church became the United Reform Church and in 1985 combined with the Methodists to become the Herne Hill United Church.

Railton Road Methodist Church
The present building dates from 1970. The first church, another iron structure, opened in 1869. This was replaced by a brick and stone structure that was severely damaged in 1940 and demolished in 1968.

St Faith's, Sunray Avenue (C of E)
The parish hall was built in 1909 and served as the church until 1957 when the present church building opened. In 1986 the parish hall became a community centre now used by many organisations. (St Faith's Church opened in 1957.)

St Philip and St James, Poplar Walk
Herne Hill's Roman Catholic Church was built in 1905 from the bequest of Frances Elizabeth Ellis. The Herne Hill Society met in the church hall from 1982 to 1992.

Dulwich Road Methodist Church (demolished)
Formerly occupying a site now a grassed area between Regent Road and Hurst Street, the church began as a temporary iron building. A permanent church was opened in 1910, but was demolished in the mid-1960s when the nearby tower blocks were built.

Herne Hill Methodist Church (Half Moon Lane/Beckwith Road demolished)
The original church on this site, built in 1900, was severely damaged by a WW2 bomb. In 1980, a block of flats, Wesley Court, was built on the site. In 1985 the congregation combined with the United Reformed Church to be the Herne Hill United Church.

Dulwich Road Methodist Church

Temple of Truth, Railton Road
The church occupies buildings converted from the original St Jude's School. It was opened in 1974 when the congregation had to move from their original premises, in Somerleyton Road, Brixton, as Lambeth Council planned to build a housing estate on the site.

New Testament Church of God, Guernsey Grove
The first church on this site, established in the early 1900s, was a small wooden shack housing St John the Evangelist Church (C of E). This was later replaced by a temporary iron church and the foundation stone to the present building was laid in June 1911. The New Testament Church of God purchased the building in 1975.

St Jude's, Dulwich Road (Cof E, now closed)
When opened in 1868, the church was designed to accommodate a thousand people. It was rebuilt after a severe fire in 1923, but suffered extensive bomb damage during WW2. After the war it was partly re-opened, but became redundant in 1978. It was used as a furniture warehouse for several years, and is currently in use as a publisher's offices.

St Jude's, Dulwich Road

SPORT, LEISURE AND ENTERTAINMENT

Brockwell Lido

Built by the London County Council, this art deco open-air swimming pool opened in 1937. In recent years use had declined. However, following a strenuous user campaign, the Grade II listed building was restored and extended, and reopened in 2007. It now offers a restaurant as well as a wide range of health and fitness activities all year round.

The fountain at Brockwell Lido. Now removed.

Brockwell Park

Herne Hill has never had its own purpose-built theatre, concert or dance hall, but the gap was partly filled by entertainments held in the park. Regular performances were given from the bandstand. Now sadly no more, this stood close to Brockwell Hall but was demolished in the 1930s. It was replaced in the 1940s by an open-air theatre with a covered stage where plays and musicals were performed. It was from here that, until the 1960s, orchestras played for open-air evening dances. More recently this tradition of plays has been revived, although the theatre stage has long gone.

It is said that in the 1920s there were 13 cricket pitches, with crowds of up to 1,500 attending matches. The Lambeth Country Show was inaugurated in 1974 and still continues. Held over a July weekend, the Show offers arts, crafts, food, drink, music and entertainment and attracts over 120,000 visitors.

Carnegie Library

The Dunfermline-born American steel magnate and philanthropist Andrew Carnegie supplied the funds to build the library on Herne Hill Road, which opened in 1906. The building was listed Grade II in 1981. Threatened with closure in 1999, it was saved by a local campaign. As well as books and IT facilities, the library has a popular children's section and art gallery.

Carnegie Library

Cinemas

Herne Hill's first cinema opened in one of the railway arches near the railway bridge and just behind what is now the Norwood Road parade. It was a rather make-shift affair with the audience sitting on long wooden benches to see short programmes of silent films. The area's first and only purpose-built cinema was the Herne Hill Cinema, at 222 Railton Road. It opened in December 1913. By 1921 the name had been changed to Cinema Grand and, in 1953, to the Pullman Cinema. At the end of the 1950s it became a bingo club, finally closing in 1986. Only the building's original façade now remains.

Herne Hill Cinema

Herne Hill Harriers

This famous athletics club was founded in a shop at 99 Milkwood Road. A group of local boys who used to meet there decided to establish the club in the winter of 1888-89. Later they moved their headquarters to the Milkwood Tavern and then to other pubs in the area. Races were organised round local roads, with track and field events using London County Council grounds and the Herne Hill Velodrome. In 1937, seeking better facilities more appropriate to one of the UK's most famous athletic clubs, operations were moved to Tooting. Recent Olympians include long-jumper Jade Johnson.

Herne Hill Velodrome

Perhaps the world's oldest purpose-built cycling stadium, the Velodrome was opened in 1891 on a site off Burbage Road. It is said to have attracted crowds of up to 20,000 in its heyday. The stadium also incorporated a running track, cinder pitch and a grass pitch for rugby and football. However it was best known as a leading venue for cycling and was used in the 1948 Olympic Games. In recent years the stadium has become run down, with its future in doubt. However at the time of writing a strong campaign is being waged to ensure its future. Triple Olympic champion Bradley Wiggins started racing here, aged 12.

Temple Bowling Club

The club, based originally in Camberwell, was founded in 1881 by a group of local businessmen. In 1913 it moved to a site on Denmark Hill and, in

Herne Hill Velodrome

1931, to its current location in Sunset Road. At first it shared the site with a tennis club but now offers croquet. The present pavilion and indoor facilities, designed by Kemp and Tasker (who also designed Dorchester Court), were completed in 1933.

Temple Bowling Club

PUBLIC HOUSES

Public houses can be an important part of an area's history and character. People often give directions to places by invoking the name of a prominent pub and bus stops are often called after a nearby pub, in a way that does not apply to cafes or restaurants. Listed below are Herne Hill's licensed pubs, past and present.

The Britannia, 233 Railton Road (closed)
A beer-house stood on this site from the 1830s until it closed in the 1930s, when the property was converted to residential use.

The Commercial, 210-212 Railton Road
A beer retailer originally occupied the site, but by 1876 the Commercial Hotel had been built on the site of 212. In 1938 the pub was enlarged by incorporating the next-door hairdresser's at 210. Prominently situated opposite the station, the Commercial is an interesting Victorian building, with a small garden, and well used by locals.

The Florence, 133 Dulwich Road
This was originally called the Railway Tavern when built in the 1860s, renamed The Brockwell Park Tavern in c1892 and enlarged to incorporate the shop next door around 1936. The name was later changed to Ganley's, and again in 2007 to the Florence. It is particularly popular with families with an out-door space and facilities for children. It incorporates a micro-brewery.

Hamilton Arms, 128 Railton Road (closed)
This began life as a beer-house in the mid 1860s and was rebuilt during the 1930s in an attractive art deco style. The pub closed in *c* 2005 and the building is now a small supermarket. The Society tried to get the building listed without success, but fortunately, many of the original art deco features have been retained.

Hamilton Arms

Milkwood Tavern, Milkwood Road (demolished)
First opening for business in 1876, the Milkwood Tavern stood on the corner of Milkwood Road and Heron Road. The pub was a centre for the local community until it closed in 1966. Part of the Michael Tippett School now stands on the site.

Prince Regent, 69 Dulwich Road
The original pub was built in the 1820s, by the side of the River Effra. It is the second oldest in Herne Hill, with the present building dating from the 1860s. The society has submitted this pub for inclusion on a list of "locally listed" buildings. It has particularly fine external plaster work and an interesting tiled roof.

Half Moon Tavern, 10 Half Moon Lane
Herne Hill's oldest pub, the building is listed Grade II*. There has been an inn here since the 17th century, although the photo shows the pub that was demolished to make way for the present building, which dates from 1896 and is the third on this site. The interior boasts some fine mirrors, cut glass and wooden screens.

Half Moon Tavern c1880 before being rebuilt.

SOME FAMOUS RESIDENTS

Sir Henry Bessemer (**1813-98**), engineer and inventor of the Bessemer Process for making steel, lived in a mansion on a large estate on a site at 165 Denmark Hill, from 1863 until his death.

James Callaghan (**1912-2005**), former Prime Minister, lived at 7 Carver Road for a time in 1967, after he had resigned as Chancellor in the Harold Wilson government and had to give up his official residence at 11 Downing Street.

James Callaghan

Henry Havelock Ellis (**1859-1939**), the writer and sexologist, lived with his secretary, Françoise Lafitte Cyon, at 24 Holmdene Avenue from 1929 to 1938.

Ida Lupino (**1918-95**), a member of the famous Lupino theatrical family, was born at 33 Ardbeg Road. Moving to Streatham in 1930, she left in 1933 for Hollywood and a successful career as a film star and director.

Freddie Mills (**1919-65**), the world light-heavyweight boxing champion came to live at 186 Denmark Hill shortly after his marriage in July 1948. After retirement, he became a popular celebrity and charity worker. Freddie's death from a gunshot wound was never properly explained.

Sax Rohmer (**1883-1959**), the author best known for creating the character Dr Fu-Manchu, moved to 51 Herne Hill in 1911 and stayed there until 1921, during which time he wrote 15 novels. There is a Blue Plaque on the house by the front door in Danecroft Road.

John Ruskin (**1819-1900**), writer, artist and social critic, came to live at 28 Herne Hill in 1823 with his father (a sherry importer) and mother. In 1842. The family moved to a larger house at 163 Denmark Hill. In 1852, with his wife Effie Gray, he went to live at 30 Herne Hill, but left two years later when the marriage broke up.

John Ruskin

Sir Mortimer Wheeler (1890-1976), archaeologist, Fellow of the Royal Society and early television personality, came to live at 16 Rollscourt Avenue when his parents bought the house in 1908, and lived there until 1924. Sir Mortimer's parents remained in the house until 1936.

Bransby Williams (1870-1961), actor, was particularly known for his portrayals of Dickens' characters. He first came to Herne Hill in 1938, to a flat at 57 Rutland Court, Denmark Hill. During the war, along with the actress Kathleen Saintsbury, he moved to Abbey Mansions, the currently derelict building behind 381 Milkwood Road, where he stayed until he died.

Roddy McDowell (1928-98), was born at 204 Herne Hill Road. Becoming an actor, he went on to star in many films on both sides of the Atlantic. He is perhaps best known for his role in the original version of *Planet of the Apes.*

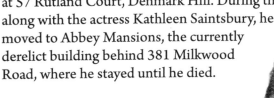

Roddy McDowell

Further information on these and 136 other famous, infamous or interesting people who lived in Herne Hill can be found in the book *Herne Hill Personalities*, published by the Herne Hill Society.

ILLUSTRATION CREDITS

Page	Credit
Cover	Aerial Photograph: ©Infoterra Ltd and Bluesky Intl Ltd, special thanks to Nathalie Hubbard for her advice. For the period map, thanks to Anthony Craig of *mappalondon.com*. The map shows Herne Hill from 1862.
4	*British Rail Southern Region sign*, courtesy John Brunton
5	Detail from John Rocque: *An Exact Survey of the Citys of London, Westminster, ye Borough of Southwark, and the Country near Ten Miles round*, 1746. Courtesy of The British Library Board.
6	*A New and Accurate Survey of the Country about the Cities of LONDON, and WESTMINSTER and the Borough of Southwark for 15 miles in Length & 12 in Depth*, engraved by Bennost (1758). Courtesy of the British Library Board.
7	*Sir Thomas Wyatt* (unknown artist) © National Portrait Gallery London.
8	*James Edward's Companion from London to Brighthelmstone* c1801, courtesy of the Society of Antiquaries of London.
9	*Casina House, Dulwich*, Drawn and Engraved by John Hassall. Courtesy of Southwark Collections, *www.southwarkcollections.org.uk*.
10	*Brockwell Hall, Brockwell Park*, Courtesy of Lambeth Archives, *www.landmark.lambeth.gov.uk*.
11	*Herne Hill Villas*, Courtesy of Lambeth Archives
12	*Herne Hill from Half Moon Lane*, 1823. Lithograph by T M Baynes. Courtesy of Lambeth Archives.
13	*Herne Hill Station*, "Building News", I May, 1863.
15-16	Courtesy of The Peabody Trust, *www.peabody.org.uk*.
17	*Trams in Norwood Road*, Courtesy of the Patricia Jenkyns Collection.
18	*Trams in Milkwood Road*, Courtesy Middleton Press.
19	*King's College Hospital*, Courtesy of the Patricia Jenkyns Collection.
20	*Flocks of sheep grazing in Brockwell Park*, Courtesy of Lambeth Archives.
20	*Memorial in St John's and the Lych Gate Memorial, Peabody Estate*, John Brunton.
21	*Sunray Estate, c 1920*, Courtesy of Southwark Collections.
22	*Bomb Damage* Courtesy of Lambeth Archives.
23	*Herne Hill Junction Today*, Photo by John Brunton.
24	*The Main Walk, Brockwell Park*, Courtesy of Lambeth Archives.
27	*Jessop Road School*, 1937. Courtesy of London Metropolitan Archives.
28	*St Paul's Church, Herne Hill. 1844*, Courtesy of Southwark Collections.
29	*Dulwich Road Methodist Church*, Drawing by Don Bianco.
30	*St Jude's Church*, Unaccredited pen drawing, 1868.
31	*Brockwell Park Lido*, Courtesy of Lambeth Archives.
32	*Carnegie Library*, Courtesy of Lambeth Archives.
33	*Herne Hill Cinema*, Courtesy of Tony Moss.
34	*Velodrome Poster*, Courtesy of Southwark Local History Studies Library. *Temple Bowling Club*, John Brunton. *Herne Hill Velodrome*, Courtesy of Southwark Local History Studies Library, *local.history.library@southwark.gov.uk*
35	*Hamilton Arms*, Courtesy of Lambeth Archives.
36	*The Half Moon Public House*, c1880. Courtesy of Lambeth Archives.
38	Roddy McDowell as "Cornelius" in *Planet of the Apes*, Getty Images.

INDEX

INDEX CONTINUED

FURTHER READING

Herne Hill Personalities	The Herne Hill Society	£5
Brockwell Boy	Jeffrey Rumble	£2
Historic Ordnance Survey maps *List of maps* (Word format)	Alan Godfrey Maps	£2
Old Map of Herne Hill 1823 (A4)	printed by John Smallwood	£1
Ways into Brockwell Park	Peter Bradley	£5
Out of the Blue 1937-2007: *A Celebration of Brockwell Park Lido*	Peter Bradley with others	£6
Herne Hill Stadium to Herne Hill Velodrome	John Watts	£5
Dulwich: the Home Front	Brian Green	£5
Dulwich: a History	Brian Green	£12
Dulwich Park	Liz Johnson	£7
Lambeth 1950-1970	Beryl Barrow	£10
Lambeth in the 20th Century	Sue McKenzie	£15
Nature Conservation in Lambeth	London Ecology Unit	£5
What to do when the Air Raid Siren Sounds	Jon Newman & Nilu York	£10
A Brixton Boy in WW2	Bill Joscelyne	£2.5
Black British: a celebration	Norman Williamson, ed.	£4.50
Lambeth Unearthed	Graham Gower & Kevin Tyler	£5
Lambeth's Edwardian Splendours	Edmund Bird	£7
The Roupells of Lambeth	Judy Harris	£5

FURTHER READING CONTINUED

Home Secrets: Tracing Your Lambeth House History	L. B. of Lambeth	£5
Reading the Riot Act	John Salway	£3
Streatham in the 20th Century	P. Loobey & J.W. Brown	£10
No Stone Unturned: The Story of a Streatham Suffragette	Anne Ward	£2.50
Southwark, An Illustrated History	Leonard Reilly	£7
Obsession: A Life in Wireless	Gerald Wells	£6

All these books can be obtained from
The Herne Hill Society, via post at:
Publications,
PO Box 27845,
London SE24 9XA
or our website at: *www.hernehillsociety.org.uk*
The Herne Hill Society always welcomes new members. New membership
enquiries, via post, at:
Membership Secretary
The Herne Hill Society
PO Box 27845
London SE24 9XA